my first book of questions and answers

things that grow

Sue Nicholson

p

This is a Parragon Book
This edition published in 2003

Parragon
Queen Street House
4 Queen Street
Bath BA1 1HE, UK

Produced by

David West Children's Books
7 Princeton Court
55 Felsham Road
Putney
London SW15 1AZ

British Library Cataloguing-in-Publication Data

A catalogue record for this book is available from the British Library.

ISBN 0-75259-828-7

Printed in China

Designers
Aarti Parmar, Rob Shone, Fiona Thorne

Illustrators
Gilly Marklew, Sarah Smith (SGA)

Cartoonist
Peter Wilks (SGA)

Editor
James Pickering

CONTENTS

Where do plants live?

Plants live everywhere! They grow in towns and cities, in the countryside, in streams, lakes and rivers, and by the sea. Some plants can live where we cannot. Cacti survive in hot, dry deserts, and some tiny flowering plants live at the top of freezing cold mountains.

How many kinds of plants are there?

There are around 400,000 different kinds of plants. They come in all sorts of shapes and sizes from tiny lichens that grow on rocks, beautiful flowers, and towering trees that reach towards the sky.

TRUE OR FALSE?

Plants live in the sea.

TRUE. Marine, or sea, plants include lots of different kinds of seaweed, such as kelp and sea lettuce.

Trees are the biggest plants.

TRUE. Coast redwood trees in California, USA, are the tallest plants in the world. They can grow more than 100 m high.

What is a plant?

A plant is a living thing, just like you. Like all living things, plants grow, breathe, feed and make babies. Unlike animals, green plants can use their leaves, roots, stems and flowers to make the food they need to grow. Mushrooms and other fungi aren't plants because they don't need sunlight to grow.

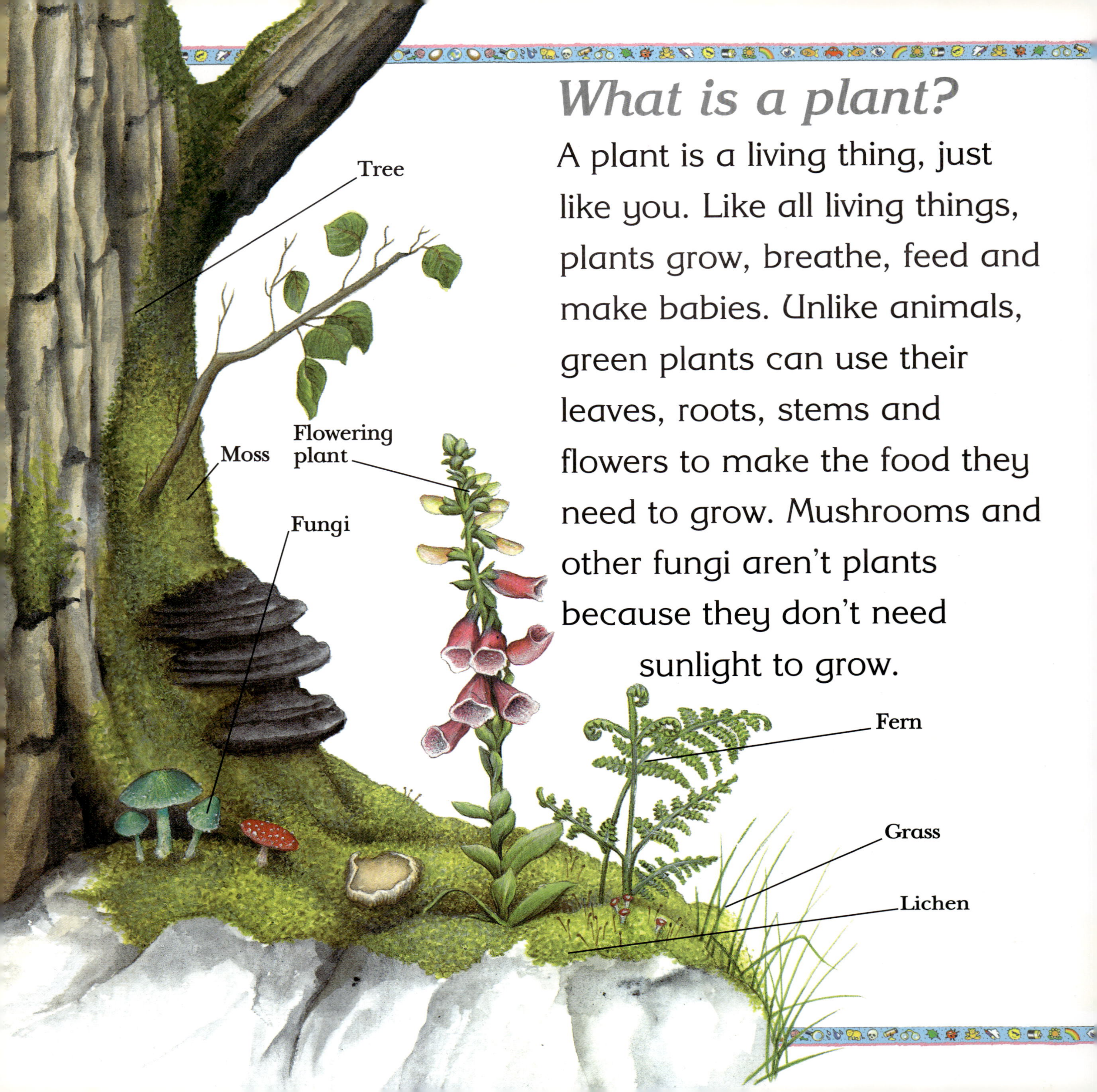

Why do plants have roots?

A plant needs roots to hold it in the soil so that it doesn't blow over in the wind. Tall trees need longer, stronger roots than small flowering plants. Roots also suck up water from the soil and carry it up the trunk or stem to the rest of the plant.

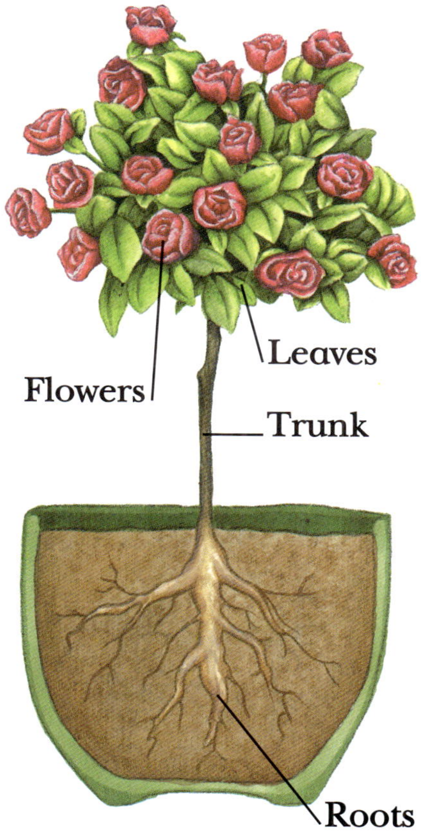

What do plants need to grow?

Plants need sunlight, water, air and space to grow. Most plants will die if they are left in the dark or uprooted from damp soil.

TRUE OR FALSE?

Every plant has roots in the soil.

FALSE. Some plants grow on other plants, not in the soil. These plants are called epiphytes. They include beautiful orchid flowers.

Plants are able to move.

TRUE. Plants don't walk or run but they do move as they grow. Some climbing plants twist around other plants as they grow upwards.

Why do plants have leaves?

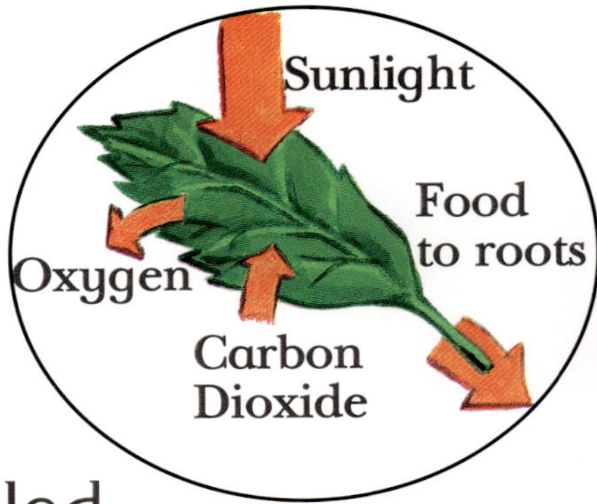

Because leaves work hard, making food for the plant to grow. Green leaves contain a green colouring called chlorophyll. The chlorophyll uses sunlight and a gas from the air, called carbon dioxide, to change water into a kind of sugar. The sugar feeds the plant. This way of making food is called photosynthesis.

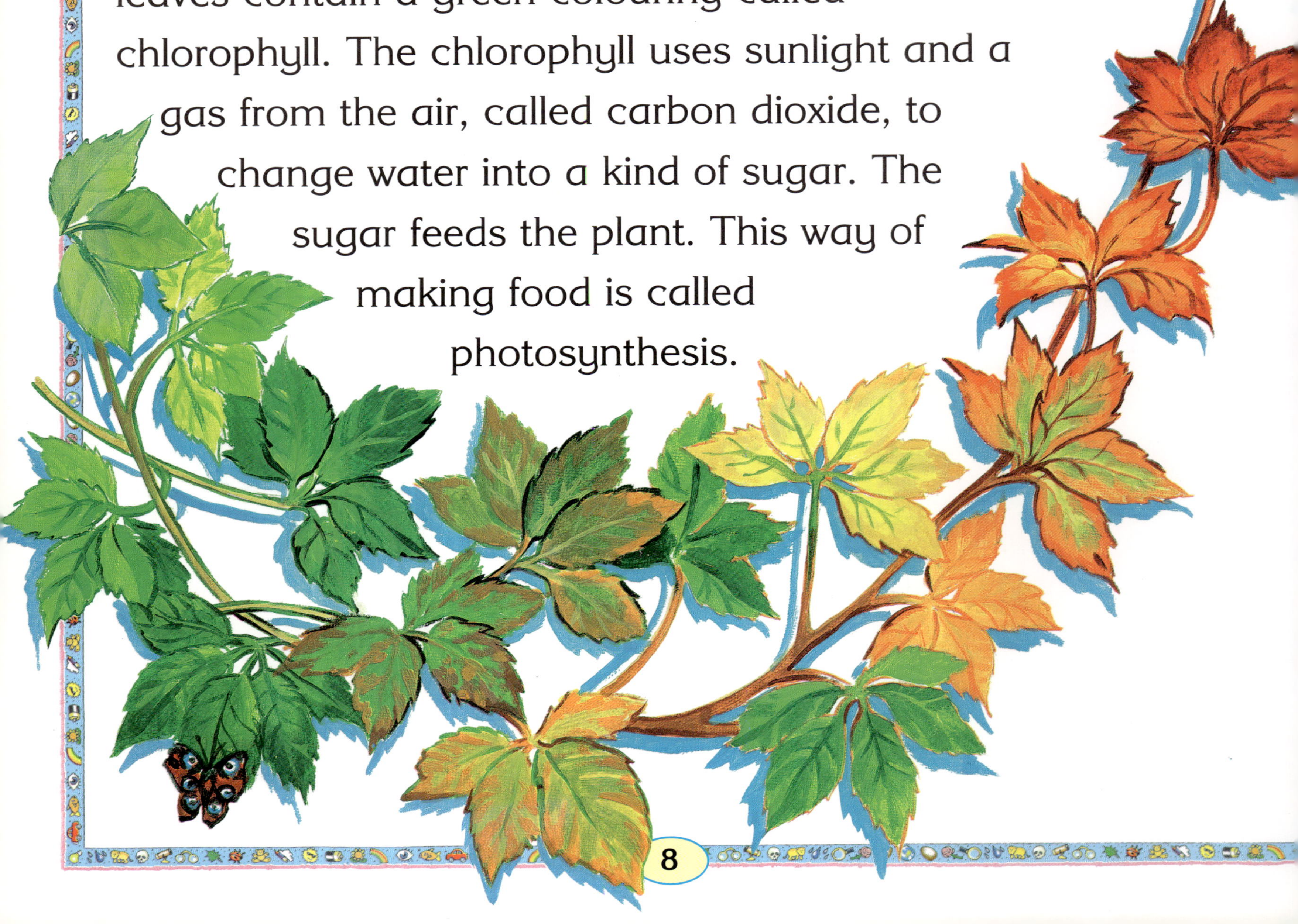

Why do some leaves change colour in the autumn?

Green leaves change colour when their green colouring, or chlorophyll, breaks down. Other colours then show through and the leaves look brown, red or yellowy gold.

Why do plants have stems?

Stems grow towards the sunlight and support the plants' leaves, so that they can make food. Stems also carry water, minerals and sugary food (called sap) around the plant. Some plants have straight stems, others are curly.

TRUE OR FALSE?

All trees have leaves.

FALSE. The saguaro cactus is a leafless tree. Instead of leaves, it has chlorophyll in its thick, green stems, which make food and store water.

Plants sweat.

TRUE. During photosynthesis, plants give off water. Just look at the water on the windows of a greenhouse!

Why do trees lose their leaves?

Some trees lose their leaves in the wintertime when there is less sunlight and water freezes in the ground. These trees, called deciduous trees, rest during the winter. They store enough food during the summer to keep themselves alive until the following spring when new leaves grow.

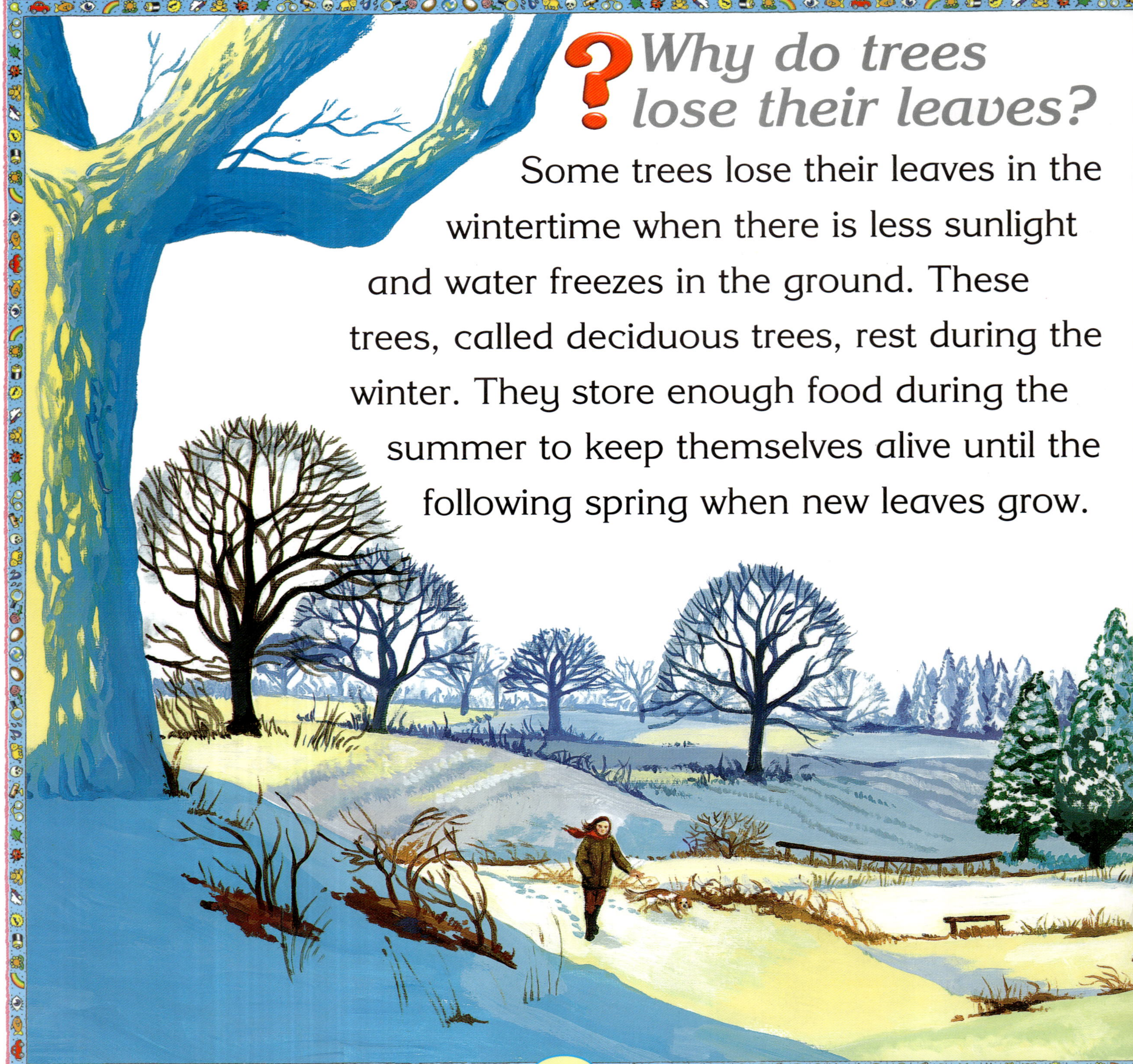

What are growing rings?

A growing ring is added to a tree's trunk every year. The ring is thick if the tree has grown a lot during a warm, long summer with plenty of rain, and thin if the tree has not grown much because the weather has been harsh.

Do all trees lose their leaves?

No – some trees keep their leaves all year round. They are called evergreens because they are always, or forever, green. They include spruces and pine trees.

TRUE OR FALSE?

Plants sleep.

TRUE. Green plants can only make food during the day when there's lots of sunlight. At night, they shut down and have a rest.

Some trees are ancient.

TRUE. The giant sequoia can live for over 2,000 years. Some bristlecone pines are over 4,500 years old! They're the world's oldest trees.

? Why do plants have flowers?

Most plants have colourful flowers to attract birds, bats and lots of different kinds of insects, such as beetles, butterflies and bees. These animals help the plants make seeds to grow new plants.

Why do flowers smell?

Sweet-smelling flowers help to attract animals. The scent tells insects and other animals that the flower contains a sweet, sugary juice called nectar which the animals like to drink.

How are seeds made?

Flowers have male parts called stamens and female parts called carpels. The stamens make tiny grains of pollen. The carpels contain eggs, called ovules. Seeds are made when the pollen reaches the ovules. This is called pollination.

TRUE OR FALSE?

All flowers smell sweet.

FALSE. The rafflesia plant smells like rotten meat! This attracts flies that like pongy smells.

Some flowers open at night.

TRUE. The evening primrose opens its petals at night and lets out a sweet scent to attract night-flying moths.

? How do insects help flowers?

Insects help to pollinate flowers by carrying pollen from the carpels of one flower to the ovules of another flower. When a bee feeds on the sweet nectar in a flower, pollen sticks to the bee's furry body. The pollen brushes off on to the next flower visited by the bee.

Why do some birds drink from flowers?

Some birds like to drink nectar, too. The hummingbird sucks up nectar through its long straw-like beak. As it feeds, its head brushes against the flower's pollen grains.

Which flowers do bats like?

Some bats like to feed on the bird of paradise flower. The part of the plant that makes pollen is flat for the bat to perch on.

TRUE OR FALSE?

Pollen is tiny.

TRUE. Pollen grains are so small that 50 or so would fit on the head of a pin!

All plants need animals for pollination.

FALSE. Some plants, such as goosegrass, pollinate themselves. Sometimes the wind blows dry pollen on to the female parts of nearby plants. This happens with most grasses and trees.

How many seeds are in each fruit?

Some fruits, such as peaches, mangoes and avocadoes, contain just one large seed inside a hard stone. Other fruits, such as oranges, lemons, apples and pears, contain several seeds called pips. Berries have lots of tiny pips around the outside of each fruit.

How do plants look after their seeds?

Many seeds have hard coats or cases to protect them as they grow. Some plants also have tasty, colourful fruits growing around their seeds. Animals eat the seeds along with the fruit. This helps to spread the seeds.

Inside an avocado

TRUE OR FALSE?

Tomatoes are vegetables.

FALSE. Many people think that tomatoes, cucumbers and peas are vegetables but they are really fruit because they all contain seeds.

Nuts are seeds.

TRUE. Nuts are seeds covered by a hard or spiky shell.

Which seeds can fly?

Some small, light seeds float in the air. Sycamore seeds have wings. Dandelion seeds have tiny parachutes. Other seeds are round and heavy so that they drop to the ground and roll away from their parent to get enough space to grow.

How do animals help to spread seeds?

When animals eat fruit they may spit out the seeds or the seeds pass through the animal and fall to the ground as droppings. Sometimes seeds with tiny hooks or spines stick to an animal's fur and are carried a long way before they fall.

TRUE OR FALSE?

Plants explode.

TRUE. Some plants, such as poppies or honesty, have seed case pods. The pods explode, sending the seeds flying.

Seeds can float.

TRUE. Coconut seeds drop into the sea and sail a long way to reach land. Each big seed contains food for a new coconut plant to grow.

What do seeds need?

Like large plants, seeds need light, air, water and space to grow. Seeds mostly grow in spring, when the soil warms in the sun and there is plenty of rain. Some seeds are planted on purpose by people to grow flowers, fruit and vegetables.

How do seeds grow?

The seed swells up in damp soil until its seed case bursts. A tiny root then pushes down into the soil and a thin shoot pushes up towards the light. When a seed starts to grow, we say it germinates.

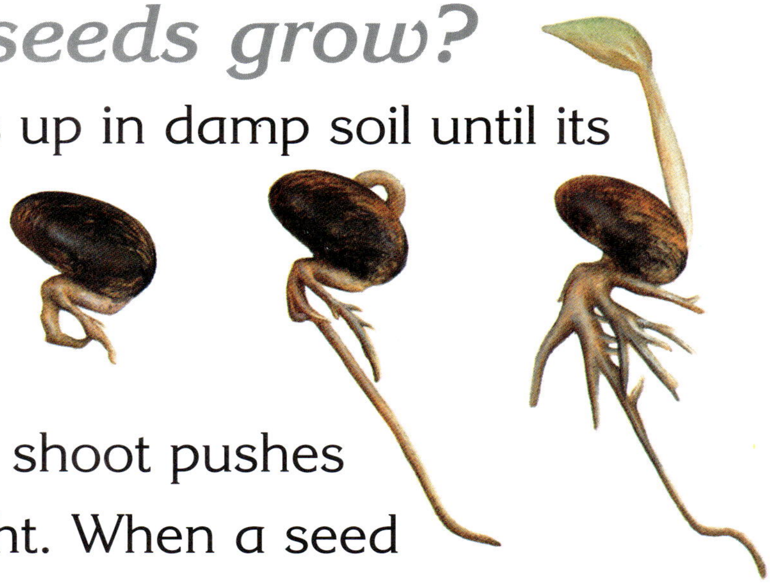

Which plants are fun to grow?

Marigolds, nasturtiums, peas, beansprouts and mustard and cress are all easy and fun to grow from seeds. You can even grow a plant from a carrot top!

TRUE OR FALSE?

Roots grow from seeds first of all.

TRUE. Roots grow first to take in water from the soil. Shoots and stems then grow from the other end of the seed.

Seeds need to grow quickly.

FALSE. Some seeds that grow in the desert can wait years for the rains to come before they can grow.

Do all plants have seeds?

Many flowering plants use their seeds to spread but some also use their bulbs, roots or stems. Daffodil and tulip bulbs make lots of tiny baby bulbs. Each bulb produces a new flower. Tubers and rhizomes are underground roots or stems swollen with food. We eat some tubers, such as potato and carrot tubers.

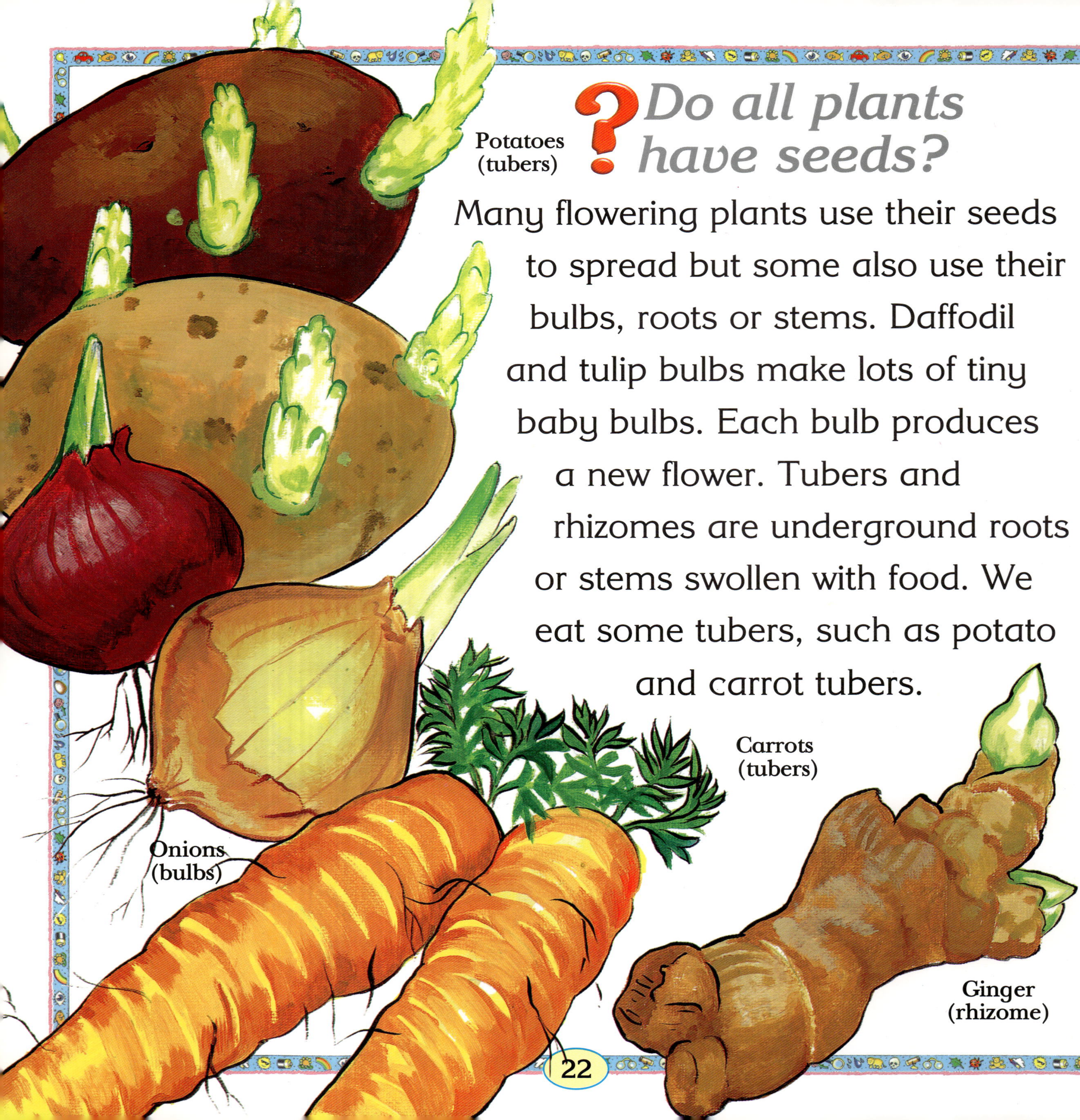

Which plants have runners?

Plants such as wild strawberries have long stems called runners that stretch down into the soil. New roots and shoots grow from each runner then the runner rots away.

What are spores?

Spores are tiny, dust-like specks made by lichens, mosses or ferns. These plants don't have flowers or seeds. Instead, the spores fly away to make new plants.

TRUE OR FALSE?

You can eat some bulbs.

TRUE. Onions and garlic are two kinds of bulb you can eat. But other bulbs, such as daffodils and tulips, would poison you.

Potatoes really have eyes.

TRUE. But not eyes like yours! Potato eyes are tiny buds, which grow into new potato plants.

? Which plants live in fresh water?

Freshwater plants grow in ponds, lakes, rivers and streams. Most have roots which anchor them in mud at the bottom. Their stems grow through the water and their leaves and flowers open above the water's surface.

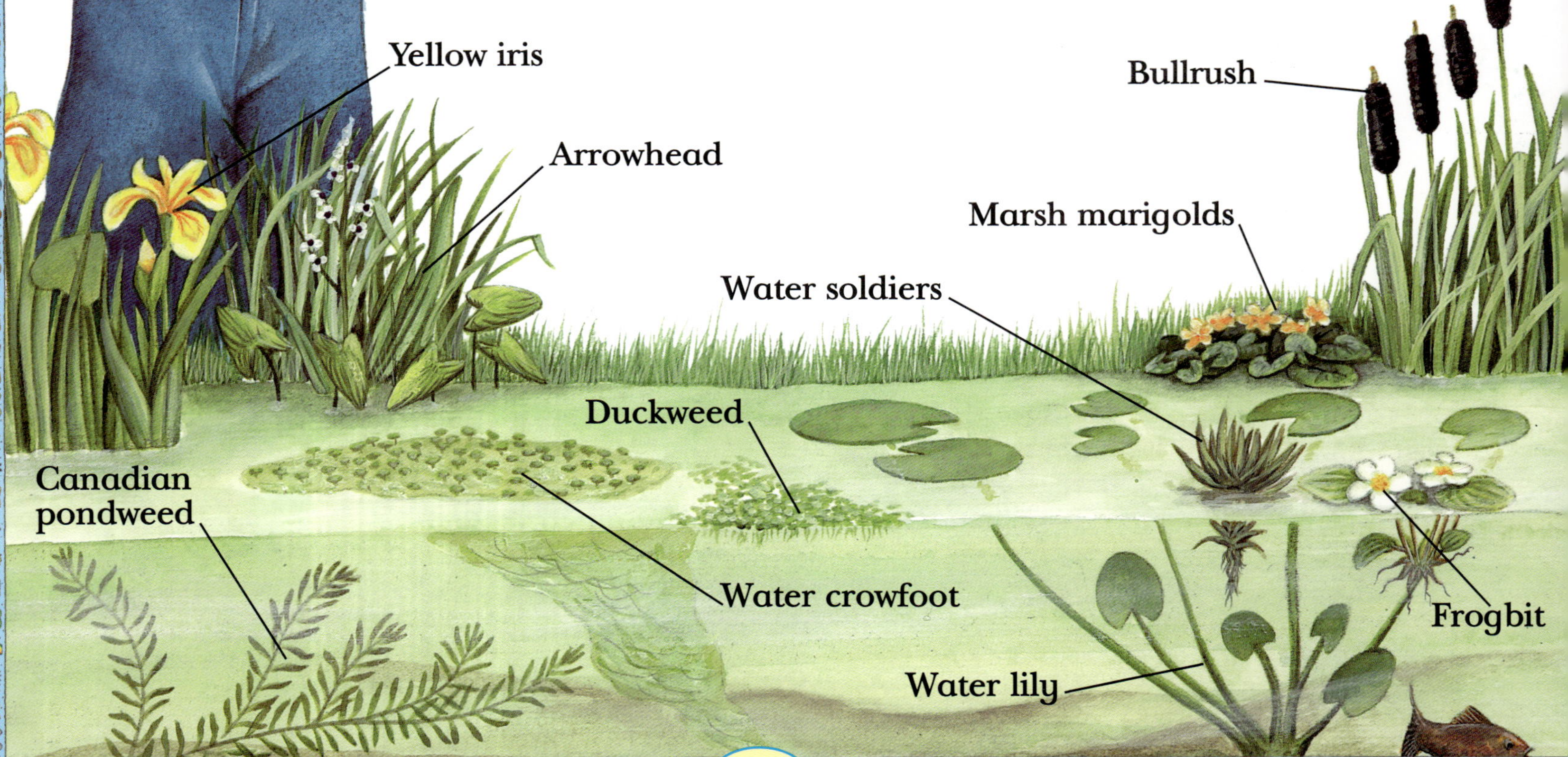

Which plants live in sea water?

Seaweeds do not have roots. Instead they fasten on to rocks using a structure called a holdfast.

Seaweed is a kind of plant called alga that lives in salty water. Algae can be red, brown, green or blue but they still contain chlorophyll for making food from sunlight. Some seaweeds fasten themselves on to rocks. Others have bubbles of air in their leaves so they can float.

TRUE OR FALSE?

Water plants often have two kinds of leaves.

TRUE. Leaves below the water are often small to avoid water damage. Leaves above are larger, to catch the light.

Seaweed can grow as tall as trees.

TRUE. Kelp can grow up to 200 metres long! Forests of kelp grow near California.

Are some plants dangerous?

Some plants are poisonous to stop animals eating them. Poisonous plants include foxgloves, lupins, deadly nightshade and belladonna. Poison ivy may leave blisters if it touches bare skin. Nettles have tiny hairs on their leaves that inject you with poison if you brush against them.

Which plants have weapons?

Brambles and roses have thorns, cacti have sharp spines and holly has spiky leaves, to stop animals eating them.

Which plants eat meat?

Some plants eat insects as well as making their own food. When an insect touches a delicate hair on the inside of the leaves of a Venus flytrap, the leaves snap shut, trapping the insect inside. Insects landing on the edge of the pitcher plant slip into a pool of liquid at the bottom and drown.

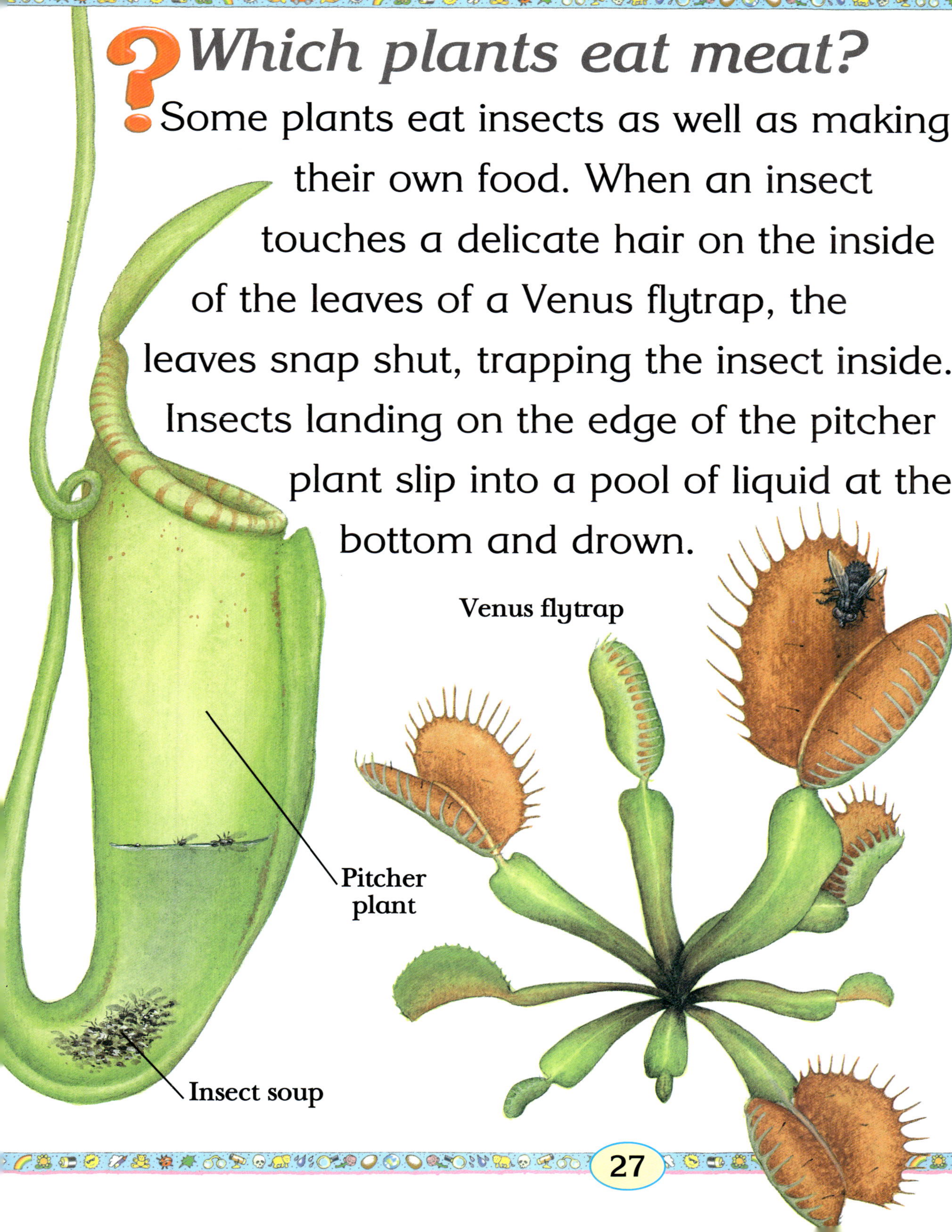

Venus flytrap

Pitcher plant

Insect soup

TRUE OR FALSE?

Some poison can be good for us.

TRUE. In small doses, the poison contained in the foxglove plant can be used as medicine to help people who have weak hearts.

Potatoes are poisonous.

TRUE. But only the leaves. The tubers are fine to eat.

Which plants can we eat?

We can eat all sorts of plants. We eat the leaves, roots and stalks of vegetable plants and all kinds of fruits and nuts. Sugar, spices, cereals (such as wheat and barley) and even chocolate come from plants.

? How do plants help us?

Plants give us lots of other things as well as food. Cotton cloth comes from the cotton plant and linen comes from a plant called flax. Plants are also used to make oil, beauty products and medicines.

Eucalyptus
(cold cures)

Oil seed rape
(machine oil)

Cotton
(clothes)

Seaweed
(photographic film)

Aloe vera
(face creams)

Foxglove
(heart medicine)

TRUE OR FALSE?

Plants give us good ideas.

TRUE. The burdock plant has tiny hooked spines. It gave us the idea for Velcro fasteners on clothes, shoes and bags.

This book was really made from plants.

TRUE. Books are made from paper. Most paper comes from trees.

Are plants in danger?

Plants are in danger from forest fires, pollution from car exhaust fumes and smoking factory chimneys. Building new homes and roads is also dangerous for the places where many plants live and grow.

Why are jungles in danger?

Jungles are in danger of being destroyed forever because so many trees are being cut down for wood or to clear land for farming. When this happens, many kinds of plants and animals may die out.

Can I help to protect plants?

Yes – don't pick wild flowers, especially in nature reserves. Try to grow a tree in your garden or in a park, or sow your own wild garden from seeds.

TRUE OR FALSE?

Trees grow again if they are cut down.

TRUE. But very slowly. It takes hundreds of years for a whole forest to regrow. More than 400 types of plant die out every year.

Plants harm other plants.

TRUE. The strangler fig winds around a tree as it grows, until eventually the tree dies.

Index